More Praise for Lexa Hillyer and *Acquainted with the Cold*

"In *Acquainted with the Cold* we are introduced to an important new voice in poetry. Lexa Hillyer's poetic gifts and ambitions are fierce. Full of vivid imagery and memorable music, these poems surprise, move, and sing. I feel I have been waiting a long time to read this wonderful collection."

—Laura Kasischke, author of *Space, in Chains*

"Charged with apt and astonishing metaphors, reckless intelligence, unnerving passion, and the 'waa waa / and the oooo waa' of their own original music, these poems race towards you, 'unstoppable,' and then, wonderfully, linger, persist like 'held fire,' so you can walk about in them and marvel how Lexa Hillyer brings everything together in this remarkable debut collection. Truly, *Acquainted with the Cold* is a book of wonders."

—Theodore Deppe, author of *Orpheus on the Red Line*

"What lasts? What ossifies? What shakes one's stupor? What transmutes? These are a sample of the intriguing concerns found in this debut collection. Lexa Hillyer, with an ear for lyrical sounds and tough questions, asks the reader to join her where imagery meets issue: 'When a whale leaps from the water's crescents/has he breached his contract with the wave?'"

—Kimiko Hahn, author of *Toxic Flora*

D1289729

ACQUAINTED WITH THE COLD
BY LEXA HILLYER

Winner of the 2011 Melissa Lanitis Gregory Poetry Prize

Bona Fide Books
Tahoe Paradise, CA

"The Life of the Foxes at Skinners Falls" by Lexa Hillyer. An earlier version appeared in *Bloodroot Literary Magazine*, 2010. Copyright © 2010 by Lexa Hillyer. Reprinted by permission.

"Inis Meain" by Lexa Hillyer. An earlier version appeared in *Spillway,* December, 2011. Copyright © 2011 by Lexa Hillyer. Reprinted by permission.

"Persephone Gone" by Lexa Hillyer. Published in the 2012 issue of *Alligator Juniper.* Copyright © 2012 by Lexa Hillyer. Reprinted by permission.

ISBN 978-1-936511-04-4
Library of Congress Control Number: 2012942209

Cover Design: Bona Fide Books
Printing and Binding: Thomson-Shore, Dexter, MI

Orders, inquiries, and correspondence should be addressed to:
    Bona Fide Books
    PO Box 550278, South Lake Tahoe, CA 96155
    (530) 573-1513
    www.bonafidebooks.com

ACKNOWLEDGMENTS

"The Life of the Foxes at Skinners Falls" appeared in the 2010 issue of *Bloodroot Literary Magazine.*

"Inis Meain" appeared in the December 2011 issue of *Spillway.*

"Persephone Gone" was a poetry finalist in the 2011 *Alligator Juniper* National Writing Contest and appears in the 2012 *Alligator Juniper* issue.

TABLE OF CONTENTS

PART ONE

PART TWO

PART THREE

PART FOUR

ACQUAINTED WITH THE COLD

Meaning? . . . Here it's snowing.
What meaning is there in that?

Three Sisters, Anton Chekhov

part one

December, the Unfinished

Your icicles' seduction slants sweet, darling—

but like the ringtone of an undialed call something lingers
off-key beneath the season's jingle, almost

imperceptible. Flitting over blasted slush,
days dart away—deceptive sparrows. Their scent:

snow. Hard breath on the window:
white. Wet. Vanishing.

A lone horn wails in a dark barroom.

These are the conditions to which you are born:
a babe in a red-lit local dive, sweat, pulse

silk-fine. Radiator's ribbon of steam
and longing: held fire. This is transmutation

I'm almost sure: wonder and night, the *waa waa*
and the *oooo waa*, stars and their imperfect light.

GHOSTING BLASKET

A cold-laced foam
             clasps me by my former ankles.
               Beach flies
              light briefly on what would be each knee—

and dizzying along the coast,
               the pang of one gull. Ongoing
                 beneath the Blasket surf:

      the kiss and crackle of barnacle,
    its false discretion
        wave-smacked, gasping.

        Fallen house, full of nettles,
            stop staring back so
            open-mouthed.

A prayer puffs up—invisible chimney—
        parts the carded
           lamb's wool clouds—absolutely nothing

        to be done. Seals bob their heads,
    sleek and certain. Like it's lonely or
          silly to have ever been human. I remember now:

    the island and mainland, their mutual curiosity.
             How the sadness of vastness used to undo me.

Heather's scattered on the hill—it's taken over—and farther off
Achill calls, all cliff and shadow.

As for my home, its stones have crumbled,
inhabited now by nettles alone—thick-stemmed, swaying.

Even rock does not last long.

BOY HUGGING AN APPLE TREE

It ossifies in me like sap, this bright
green soccer field, carved into
an apple orchard's heart—envy-angled,

childless and silent.
Our first confessions buoy
bluely as we slip

through the day drinking cabernet—
triple-hooks: argument, stain, mouth.
Branches tear at us, tangle my hair,

and the sun's tarnish, blood-rich,
smears the trees. We eat darkness—
arched

and covetous of Jonah Gold.
For the Winesaps are unripe, red-
skinned but sour white inside.

As for Empires—every one of them has fallen.

Mud, crisp air, dank earth—and rot.
Tart, sweet, sickening rot:
ants crawling over mounds of it. Then

somewhere an echo—
a boy named Leggo clings to a tree,
his round cheek pressed to the bark

or perhaps his father's calling:
let go, let go. But oh
he will not.

Bella Lago in Winter

A water-locked tribe, we suffer the whims of waterfowl, where the cumulus shadows arch: sometimes we lie sideways eyeing the wide whirlpool night, wondering if the constellations lack succulence, if that is why even when the eagle flies upside down it is only a feathery flirtation and not, as once we thought, a temptation to devour the sky.

Each year a great ceiling comes to separate us from the stars. Temperatures plummet. At first, it's an iridescent scale, so fine and bright that wild prisms imprison and free us, but soon it thickens to white, sealing us in. Stark armor. We hunker, bottom-feed, beg for sleep. A few go topsy-turvy, delirious as a ripple. Not all of us wake.

Then vibrations shake our stupor: first the tremor from above, a shrieking. Suddenly, a crack. Everything moonlit blue. We wait while lines drop and float, thin and silvery and hooked, watching bubbles glow and rise.

Some of us will bite at any bait. Some pine for the still black pond above—believe another life exists. In the icy flux of darkness and hunger, sometimes it's just beyond us to resist.

BEDROOM

Lightning. The door cracks—
a harsh florescent sliver.

The definite nudges the indefinite: soft sound
of breath in the dark, of birds quaking.

He mistook dove song for the call of loons.

Duff is the buttocks or fine coal. Burn your name
on the flesh of a cow, though everything is ash anyhow.

Coats, enclose us—keep us
from the typo of the coast—

for cold wind blows the drifting sand into a ridge of sand.

It was me. I was the one
who thought they sounded like loons.

A streak of light scathes the hollows:
skin, shadow, thunder. Cover.

ASK ME WHAT I WANT

Icicles grip the drainpipe:
hell-sharp, glinting.
Inside a small tank
an animal with very small
paws stands up against the glass
sniffing—blind
as any Oedipus. You nuzzle
me; I nuzzle you.

Earrings drop blood-red
beads. Have I written
the right word? I can't decide
anything: where your face begins
mine ends. What we've said,
what we mean. A pink mattress
skirts the wall—photographs: a mother,
her boy lost in the snow.

At the station: black,
deserted. We have our tongues
in each other's mouths; tracks
crack their jaws at us, envious.
Everything moves in its own direction—
our lives, our hands. Unseen, a train
rumbles closer, chanting
yu yu yu yu yu yu yu

TODAY IS THE DAY YOU SAID YOU'D BE BACK

and fever wakes me.
      Delicately comic-wrapped,
                a painted tile lies

          by my door—morning's
          first and hottest light: a girl
              resting, head on knees;

    her long hair streaks through
psychedelic blue—skyward
the birds dart, sparkling.

        Turn east. Bicyclists.
        Otherwise just this silence
          we agreed was best.

At a card table
      old men play with dominoes
            numbered just like those

    choose-your-own haikus
you scrawled on a plane in June:
their infinite un-

               decidedness. Yet
          I boil the water, watching
       and waiting, waiting

    as your tea flower
unfurls its watery heart
      in my steam-streaked glass.

THE METEOROLOGIST'S POP QUIZ

1.
A sac of fog fills the park, obscuring the city on its other side.
Budding trees prick up their pale tips. If that is your first

answer, the question was: *a house on fire.*

2.
Manic in the middle of the night, someone beats her old
Oriental rug. Like gunshots, dust clouds the marble lobby floor.

Three lines, three lines, a hole where the body should be.

3.
Basement windows shatter—a dog's cries crystallize
in our veins. This falling apart is part of the process.

4.
Supporting beam, interior wall: flurries
brush the window, winter whitening the dark.

      Inside, night claims all.

5.
Hearing the hail on the roof, whether we've made
some terrible misstep eludes us—ubiquitous, yet impossible
to suss out this vaporous not-knowing, pierced only
by the fingertips of trees:
batlike—blind dart—

6.

The skyline has gone away. These are its bones.

Hunker down, my dear, stay
clear of the burning home.

SHEEP'S LAMENT

We're the snow-effect: bodies softened
to one white. Cloud-cold
breath. A kind of disappointment.

On distant tracks a dark love whistles,
smoke-spent.
Rattle-box, betrayer—nettle-sting.

But we are the constant witness
to so much mourning
over cut clover *oh* over

black-ringed glass. We hover,
heedless
of human need—what this woolen heart

cannot comprehend—haunches
trembling as stars
herd us forever through the frozen grass.

TRINITY

1.

Trinity's gate's frozen, so a janitor's out torching the lock:
              bits of burnt paper whisking by,
                        kids on the street crying: *fire!*
              Lord of the blind, take my hand.

              Beyond my reflection
the orange and yellow seats
              of the Astoria line   flicker.   (Who are you,
       man in the red hat?)
A girl crosses the shiny road in a pink puff coat,
       then we tunnel down, and there's only my face
                                floating in darkness.

              None of it has hit me yet: dawn's just a subway car,
       night still rattling.

2.

I won't be the last
       to misunderstand—fixed
              like ice to window—to want too much

              from a man who's fucking
       some seventeen year old. In the grand scheme it seems

only of mild importance, the way we dread into being
       what we already know. But hidden. But young and afraid.

All day the avenues melt and glisten;
                parked cars in the lot linger: snow-islands—
        a shadow where one has driven off,   tire marks lengthening like
                                strands of black hair.

Hour of darkness, comb through me, come through on at least your
                                                one promise.

3.
I nod off as the bus slogs along Columbus. Always
        this same conundrum: how to describe that windowed world

part mirror, part   what lies on the other side.
                                        I'm heading home
        over knee-high snow—the wind's
                        incessant hiss—shaking

        as curbs sob off slush. All I know is
I'm not ready
        to know more. Father of lies, don't leave me.

        At the church, I press my forehead to the gate's
                        char-marked mouth.
        Flurries hurry down, dizzying—I   face them now, false
tenderness, melting. We kiss and kiss, numb-white,
                                senseless.

SONNET ABOUT A PARTY IN THE MANSION OF DECAY

Shine on, crystal flute, and bubbles, climb—
scarlet seeds tapping my teeth: tiny fines
past-life paid—while in the parlor
the five-piece plays on a parquet floor
that warps, that groans. Wind, ice-laced,
wanders disillusioned—a god alone—
winding its way up the grand staircase
where music from below mutes to stone.

It's the house itself, must be—these tall
aching walls—that makes us fear all we'd give up
for love. The twine untwisted
from an ivory napkin I tie 'round your wrist,
then wrap you in my legs in this blue dress lake:
we'll float or go down. Make no mistake.

The Life of the Foxes at Skinners Falls

This is the dance in which we're the vixens.

A fox is a Vespa: dash in the semi-dark. Scarlet branches scratching. Quick shock, breaking through ice. I'm somewhere just past White Lake Fire Company, wind cold on my ears.

The thing about a fox is the tail. The flash. Its already-gone-ness. If there's an invisible crack in the world, it's where foxes whirl through. Wolf-maned. Crab-eaters. On the other side, skulks of them: freed troops of Cozumels flitting in fields of wild chamomile. I've seen it. Those snarling Tibetan sands.

But back at Ditch Plains, the train tracks lie black in snow—funny how it's the inevitable that scares us so. So close to knowing something significant, but evening's just a list: dark, ice, river.

Beneath it all, the small talk of icicles. The *fukhs* imagined, many-named. Perhaps some gleanable fact, but Bella Lago where the river feeds is frozen too. It gleams. The moon like a dime.

We shimmy.

It's not catching the fox but sensing it that matters: something is scurrying out there.

MAY, THE PLATONIC IDEAL

Humid, pollen-spooled—still
cool and noncommittal at night

your clean magnolias open
magenta-white mouths. Mild-

mannered, maddening: I want
only more, more—

like a reservoir you're purposeful
cerulean, lily pad and petal-strewn.

Sting of grassy rain-soaked
mornings—exquisite almosts like

seed fuzz floating on air—
tree musk, moss scent, sweetest

touch . . . I feel so unsure of you—
you promise too much.

part two

TEN LIES MORE

If you betray me I shall know immediately.
If all crayons were one color then you would be purple.
If it ever stops raining I'll give rollerblading a try. Uphill and down I'll go.
When morning winks, it is winking at me.
We've shared a secret—a highly sexual secret I shan't reveal.
If clocks turned the other way, all the toast in town would burn.
Were unlove a beverage, it'd cure itself upon being drunk.
Should rivers of fire cover us, the gulls will screech, mocking.
When I quit my job, I'll be an old-fashioned pilot—those goggles!
If I had the time I would tell you everything, everything.

A Monument in Halted Cry, or the Affair

I lost my nerve. From this balcony,
this black dress, revere me:
a perfect punch cup. You know
the half-life of a metal is a

chemical change—excruciating.
All those millions of years. Call me

little mama: your weight
will tug me under. Let me be
your hazel tree—I said I'm willing
to be your willow.

Half-lit room, half-lie: I fall
down the stairs. It's all on purpose.
We're both in the backseat
on the road to god knows where.

Now it's winter and you're circling
my knees. We wear formal attire,
we hide: making out in a motel bathroom
where you let me brush your teeth.

Blinds bang against the windowpane.

Summer collides head-on
with the oncoming traffic
of families returning home.
I begin to wonder

just how much I have imagined.

Is it true—do we love
what's unstoppable,
bigger than us, what moves on
whether or not we can keep up?

You saunter down the cement walkway,
cross the street, and melt into snowfall.

I said I'm willing.

Hidden Hand

Lamps glow in a furniture store's window; stars
light up the planetarium. A midget boards the bus.

On the street, a man rolls secrets into two
falafel balls as shouts fly. A taxi squeals away:

ten lost phones warbling in his cab. I'm losing
the game—your eyes barely show

over red-backed cards . . . some bluff
too long uncalled. You soak it up—

the smoke in the air: a ghost who remembers
smoke and misses it. How we hold on.

How we fold.

Innocence in the Mission District

Nights, rain cocoons you, broken only
                     by produce trucks unloading on the street.

Avocados, orange cartons, vines of tomatoes.

All day the sun plays out its fickle
relationship with the hills—
               how you'd always almost
                      get what you want
if not for the wind
or the mind meandering
            down the back steps, out past
                the compost garden and Spanish-graffitied alley.

Magnolia, bicycle, tourist, cloud.

This city feels empty—the parks
                sparse. Passing a school,

you notice a girl and boy, brown-skinned as bark,
               tucked into the arms of a newly blossomed
                    almond tree.
They are nearly hidden, whispering, while
              all around them white petals hover
                   ready to fall.

YOU JUMP FROM A PLANE IN JULY

Conjurer of gravity: postmark, vile ink.
I thought you were afraid to dive.

Wind, shudder, mild sting. The soft skin
of your face forced back. Your hair—

*

My kite hovers over beach, waits for me
to sleep, then tears, then strays,

unreels me until there's only a white line
strangling my finger—a child's ring.

*

Dog who does not know its name, who cannot
come when I call . . . to you, I think

it's all the same:
lie down, lie down, lie down.

*

Sprawled on the sand—*stay, play dead*—
I hold the sky with a wild string.

INIS MEAIN

Waves shatter moss-green on Inis Meain—all
rock, the merest of tall weeds, grass,
magenta heather buds and buttercups in fields you cannot run across
for the stones hidden below.

And though it isn't native here, somehow
the distant waft of bergamot.

A hive hums on this side of the cliffs, over surf's
harsh hiss: honeycombed
haven divvied up by some divination like the island itself,
its meadows carved into pieces
by a maze of low-running stone walls.

Here we are helpless, split into parts.
We snug the coast close
against buffets of slanted rain. We cut
straight through the rocky green hills of bliss—all of this
at once—briars, brambles,
berry thorns, cattle-groan of blue-gray sky—too much.
Now I see why

the isle beckons those silent hook-beaked black birds
who pry its cracks one by one. Inis Meain,

undo and divide me with stone.

PATIENCE IN THE WILD CITY

You call me late at the office
        after everyone has gone.
Your voice—its taste unties me

in the semi-dark, towers outside
        my windows spotted with
penny-lights. *I'm so worried*, you say.

I can't sleep. There's a wolf out alone
        in the night, digging up
traps with her teeth . . .

Some sad old story you don't know
        the ending of. My desk
lamp flickers; a tiny plane flies over:

two insect-golden eyes. I
        tell myself it's all for good,
this almostness, what you've

furred and called *wolf*—the way you
        whirl toward me and away.
Beyond the wooden pilings

that stretch across the Hudson
        a barge blinks: *wait for it—*
whatever it is, it will come to you

partway—for the water, it flows
in either direction
and has nothing to do with want.

TAKING THE BEDS OUT OF THE ATTIC BEFORE THE STORM

August. Our truck lurches down the gravel road to the farm:
    dogs howling and chickens in a tizzy over one cock.
Moist-palmed kids hold fresh eggs. You make me ache
  to tear the rhubarb's pink stems—can't tell
    what's poison from what's not.

    Seven old beds wedged high in the hot
   attic room: you and the other boys drip
trying to slip them down a tight back stairwell.
  When one bed hitches itself to the banister,
     you hack right through its springs and fluff.

   Meanwhile, the yard listens to crickets. A puppy nibbles my fingers,
hungry for crumbs, as the sky's loose sheets rag the sun:
    the shape of things only hinted at in a pre-rain wet—

  You take my hand
 and we run through tall grass to the Isinglass edge,
 shed our shorts and
   shirts and slide into its stinging cold, clear water.
 A dog follows, pants, splashes. We kiss
   and swim until we hear thunder's
    premonition: a low, protective growl. The old pines
    whine like mares in heat.

We're held in time—holding each other—
      swollen with our own wholeness, just before the first drops fall.
      Such blind, bright faith:
          raw and white
              as an uncracked egg.

NOT THE DOLL'S VERSION

The miniature rocking chair was mysterious:
thick-veined like a maple leaf, its arms
as sturdy for standing upon as the back
of a tortoise. And it was curvaceous:
the gradations of sweetness from
seat-rim to center satisfying
as those in a jar of jam. It swayed
ever so subtly in its own wind! Yet
it was not promiscuous. Its name
was never known, but evoked by *serendipity*.
All in all, the rocking chair was a comrade
(unless you were hoping to embrace.)

But this is not the full gist of the story.
For what if you were a pair of arms?
Cradle the broken doll to get a better understanding. Just
remember her state of undress, that her pink lips are mum,
for we have a long-held pact, I and she.

MYSTERIOUS ORIGIN

Pacing through the shadows of this city I somehow
helped build but remain

inferior to, so many spontaneously
ask if I'm Russian, I may as well

agree, for this is how we create
the self out of nothing: snow

melting, voices blended. How we
long for resurrection, or how I'm charged

with your memory, permanently
scarred, the flesh appearing whiter where you've touched it

         and won't

do so again. I meet a stranger who half has your face
and kiss him in the half-light

of a bar, for hours. We lean into the mossy hill
of winter coats, which disappears beneath us

as the tribes don them and depart, carving
their separate, sickle-shaped paths home:

bridging the night in which we find ourselves
homeless, noses touching, his hair

falling over my eyes. We can't stop
erasing the ghost between our bodies, leaving

our mouths' lost words all over
one another, whoever we are.

part three

SEPTEMBER, THE WITHHOLDING

Like the shore on a gray day: un-
spoken for, all serious and scarfless

in a cardigan-button solitude,
you're a concrete cityscape, twin rivers

racing through. Summer's wiser sister,
I await your sign: curb-lit pigeons,

an overheard whisper, or a question
in the curved shape of the spine . . .

Wanderlust: my statues' eyes so
unfinished follow your loose swirl

of shopping bags, dingy white in wind. I want
your dark flying hair on my face—

Impatient and dumb, my life's a doll's dream
or the lone vertical of a stocking seam.

Caliban's Ambien Ad

Be not afeard. AMBIEN CR's approved to help you
fall asleep. The isle is full of noises, sounds and sweet
airs that give delight and hurt not, and the first layer
dissolves quickly to help you fall fast, the second slowly
so you stay asleep. Sometimes a thousand twangling
instruments will hum about your ears, and sometimes
voices after long sleep will make you sleep
again, again, again. Be not afeard. In clinical studies,
AMBIEN CR was effective for up to seven
sometimes voices. In dreaming, the clouds open,
show riches ready to ready to drop upon you. If you're
considering a sleep aid, it might be time it might be
time to ask your doctor—sounds and sweet airs—
for AMBIEN CR CR CR CR. The isle is full
of noises. It might be time be time. Be not afeard.
Stay asleep stay. Sometimes voices approved to help you
open the clouds and fall fast the first layer a twangling
of sweet airs CR CR CR and cry to dream again.

15 Texts from Vesuvius

1

Wanted to say hi, how are you, and to tell you:
this is how it is.

2

Dust settles on my palms, darkness embalms me,
the long night. It's what we

bargained for: what we always knew even when I
didn't know one single thing.

3

Hey, just checking in. FYI, she waited so she could die
on the same day Jesus died: Thursday.

4

Grampa's been asking for the porch chairs;
though it's cold-as-Christ for April, they think
it's a good sign. You can't be wholly broken

if you're planning for spring.

5

Mouth of hell, what's the reason
for your hot madness, molten
gold and black?

6

I hear the Holy Ghost trying
to ignite: first the back

burner sparks and flames on the electric
stove, a miserable, eerie smell—

then the DVD player moaning,
an otherworldly cry—

7

Listen closely. That gurgling:
there's lava in everything that moves.

8

Happy Easter! Snow flurries fall on all
the Christians scurrying from church, and the Jews

out jogging in the brisk morning air or
picking up their dry-cleaning. Pride and one

sweater have been packed up—no sense
blaming people for who they really are.

9

Magma: volatile, unpredictable, etc.
I did try, though. To be true.

10

You like to remind me of Pompeii, preserved
seventeen hundred years in ash, blurring the ink I guess
as you outline a volcanic silhouette against

the setting sun. Maybe you wonder
what you've done. Or maybe
you don't wonder about any of it.

11

I don't think this has to do with love,
though I was never much of a believer.

12

This is what we bargained for: this is it,
even though we thought there was no

bargaining involved. How's it going?
Long time no see! Cover me
in embers, harden over

my body like a rock.

13

Here's what happened: the dishwasher
with its diluvial churnings had no water: it breathed

hot air, a film of filth caked along its inner surfaces,
bits of food stuck to plates like fish scales.

14

Now everyone is sleeping,

splayed peacefully on the ground around the savior's feet.
He doesn't want to wake them; gazing up at the dewy
predawn sky, he whispers *why* . . .

Like a father—*after everything*—like a friend, it is written:
God betrays him in the end.

15

It's raining so hard. Disaster,
natural or otherwise: talk to me softly.

Who knows if we'll be saved.

WHAT WE DO

Cool, the mirror's fog—
across it I trace a prayer,
dissolving

as my reflection emerges:
Chin. Eye.
Paper cut, paper cut,

your backwards smile . . .
Both faucets leak and I don't know
if it's coincidence, or just

that the problem lies deeper—
hands raw
turning

the knob. Beads of water
shine in the sink. Through which
closed door have you

so subtly slipped? The stairs
refuse to admit
whether anyone's gone up them—Look:

a child slowly disassembles
all he's built, piling the blocks
back into their box.

Something spools out of me like thread.

Ten of Daggers, what is that
house on the hill? How you turn
your back on me.

As our walls sleep, the drip
goes on—almost inaudible,
almost an answer.

NOVEMBER, THE CURSED

Your leaves, dismantled, madly rise.

Pigeons reign over paved roofs while the black
starlings—urgent, hectic—possess

the elm. You've abandoned the branches—
their detestable nudity: too many eyes.

A bright-red scarf billows from a window
as a stranger hunches by with a laundry sack.

Breeze, I have learned these lies,

yet every time I go three days alone
I'm convinced by some dark decree that no one

comes back. And this is not the same lawless
guilt I feel toward my father, cast from the skies.

Your leaves burst forth in a terrible frenzy—
and now the red scarf comes free: it flies.

A Prophet's Lover Toes the Predawn Floor

for something absolute: he steps into
                              her jeans
                              and cannot get them off.

Barefoot on the front stoop, Tiresias—sleepless, unwhole—holds
              her bathrobe close against mist that isn't
                              rain but is, as it

doesn't fall and does. One-tenth desire. He disappears.

              Wind stirs wet branches overhead, horizon
                      rounding to birdsong's
                              high zero.

*Is this the we we
never knew we'd be?*
              Wanderer, blind interpreter, self-
                              inverter.

              Morning breathes through Tiresias's hair.
An early jogger rounds the corner.

              Stillness, take
          pity on him. Take pity on
her: *Make us into who we thought we were before.*

Ultimate Coast

Anarchy in the waterline's frozen reeds:
　　　　winter fowl battle over a beetle.

　　　　　　A hawk has her eye on us,
　　　　　　tipping past the dark ring of trees.

　　　　On the other side: only more
of this less-than-perfect cold.

Fox prints in snow: agency, urgency. They say
　　　　all energy moves toward chaos.

　　　　　　The air pales, wistful, tastes
　　　　　　of northern glaciers—

　　　　numb to its own chill.
Was there a fox here at all?

Every delicate print submits
　　　　to the entropy of snowflakes.

　　　　　　What is the difference between me
　　　　　　and that crystal-covered fir tree?

　　　　We're both reeling toward darkness,
free-floating through stars' spilt milk.

Storm Is Blind

Tonight the city is contained in a room.
Theaters all turn inside out.

The wind rages, and at street's edge
a pair of white mittens melts into snow.

*

You don't have to say everything;
you don't have to be destroyed
in order to speak. What language leaps

beyond the current—*fury, fury*—*flying fish?*

Or are all words solace of the obsessed?

*

I leap over the wet space

between cab and curb.

You loved my human sadness—held it
like an egg in your palms.

I can't see—oh, give me
what my body can't give. That may be
all I need.

*

Who is that white bear
bedless and swimming—is his

god like him? Pale fur hollow
and beneath it, skin black as the arctic night
that lasts for months . . .

*

I still don't think I know
how to fuck or to love.

Wind whips the snow.
My hands disappear.

The storm is blind—
no wonder,
no wonder it wants my eyes.

part four

PERSEPHONE GONE

Winter. Demeter's lost daughter
rides the subway. Night's stalling.
Was it deception or desire, the song
of the tongue's red tang that taught her

to count out a fistful of seeds or
to swallow them, knowing they belong
to the magnet that pulls us down
into darkness? We keep calling

it a mistake, but maybe she needs her
token, a souvenir, to leave
some part of herself there. How I'd like to believe
when I emerge from that tunnel underground—

hardly real—and float up to the street,
that a colder, steadfast me hurtles on beneath my feet.

JANUARY, THE JAILOR

Blue, blue, your sky's a billiards cue—
fading white like a cat's scratch

begun to scar. The wind's a match:
struck on, blown out as my bus rambles past

Avalon Chemists where the remedy-less
return—I guess because the way we yearn

rounds like barbed spirals on a prison
fence. God, you've stiffed this town:

a taxidermist's dream. And I am the girl
trapped in a basement with her dead mom's furs.

Just look how you double-back. You cul-de-
sac; your flurries frisk us, helix us . . . unfix

the past. A long hair curls in the drain.
I'm slipping through your slats again.

February, the Saint

Cool voice of mercy, turned down low,
lower. Knot in my throat. Ah, there you are—

my long-lost dove season; I hear your coo,
steepled with secrets like Sleepy's

Mattress Store. I don't think I can stand it anymore—
your chamber of abandoned beds. I head past

a diner called The Mansion, all those matching
checkered chances, and enter a church—

rustling pigeons' wings—where your chill echoes
in the latticework of hymn. A single feather

sifts through the many-paned sky.
Your martini's bone dry, licks its rim,

some kind of ultimatum—you know me well.
Like Sartre, you make the little things hell.

FROM THIS SIDE OF THE WATER

Once there was the absolute zero of the lake
and the soil-scented shore:
mud, memory, mountain.

Reflective waves amid rough silver firs
trap my girl, my ghost:
her face a white fist,

the wet rock of need.

Youth, beauty, you get the idea . . . Water's
no place for rage.

The air pricks, sensing snow.

I take a sharp breath, memorize the trees,
their ice-tip certainties. Then begin

to climb the slope away from her frozen body,
those pale arms wrapped in reeds.

March, the Immaculate

You're the end of so long a winter:
the bed damp and murky. Maybe

it's too late to let you in. Mud flows
through my mind, a mouthful of

distance. A window holds
the lamplight in its snare. I smell the air,

wineglass-red—stale breath of Demeter—
how well she's held me under her spell.

Her semidarkness: the veins of night
sticky, external. But that ecstasy

of isolation—I crave it—celibacy,
defining, bright! White-cold and crisp and true.

March, blow your clean sheets upon me.
You kill with all you cannot undo.

As We Forgive Those Who Trespass Against Us

i.
Tattered fence, defense torn: to transgress
is a body wrapped in barbed wire.

Two hunters step sideways softly: the convalescence
of a cold moon is turning them to deer.

The sight of untroubled twigs on the forest floor arrests
me like the first snow, which falling for no one, falls on us.

Serenely, a haunted hawk or shadow passes
like an arrow, cracking open the sky.

ii.
When a whale leaps from the water's crescents
has he breached his contract with the wave?

This much I know, baptized with dripping hair: blessed
are the amphibious, because we crave

movement. You shiver, undress,
convinced you'll be saved.

Sweetly urged, let the current possess us:
bloody, damaged, finally brave.

iii.
Who can say which one of us trespasses,
or what *misdemeanor* really means:

the language of bedsprings cannot access
or apprehend this, legs like prison keys.

You scale wet brick, crawl under the lenses
of a curtain that keeps winking.

There's a ladder pinned against our senses,
and we're climbing, and we're sinking.

iv.
No hoofprint or wingfall in flurries, just a frayed mess
of trees blanketing our indiscretion:

pale tent arched like a breeze overhead, your tresses
stand on end: a sinewed imposition . . .

latched onto branches, a spiderweb quivers, glistens.
We get down on our hands and knees and howl.

Forgive us. The woods stand still. Listen:

THE LINGUAL UNDERSTANDING OF STARLINGS

Glass (*sh*)atters, ice ratchets through the lake,

rain undoes snow 'til the snow
        surrenders. I let (*go*).

Starlings gather in the trees—it's this
thing they do, inhabiting and becoming.

Their one hundred forebears taught them the
grammar of waiting, of one

        clause (*claws tucked*)
inside another, another.

(*Sh*)iver—un(*enfold*)ed. It's just
    (*us*) now.

        (*Trust*) is an absence of
leaves (*in the wind*)—

OUR LAST NIGHT ON THE ROOF

The dome's lit on 50th.
Shabby neon eases up from
the street where buildings don
their anonymous glow;

the sky's a scattering of tiny
TV lights. This roof
lies at the center of a dark
valley, Hell's

Kitchen, midnight, the moon
furiously silver and so close
to whole. That is my leg
you hold and kiss—no simile, just

the thing itself. All of Manhattan
stares at screens: blue, twinkling . . .
Do these constructs misconstrue us?

We've either risen to this height or
we fall, but are we
lovers? So little
holds us together.

Your mouth; the back
of my knee . . .

STEAM

It rattles the carved iron lid, leaks
from my teapot's imperfect rim: damp prayer
or a snake doffing skin. Such precision,
turning its head in the chilled morning air
it twists through the thin streak
of sunlight sneaking in.

The stark porcelain in my hands glows;
dark liquid whispers a new-made word
unbidden, silent, wet, scald:
maybe a warning, so hot and blurred?
A hidden name I cannot know—
one I was born with but never called.

CHANGELING

It's the hour of faeries' stealing.   I rise
numb from underground: the countdown
          of city blocks begins. In the drizzly

          merlot dusk   this skin
tingles, and everything seems changeable.

Only a moment ago I fed a smirking crocodile,
my face floated pale amid pop ash
at the base of a bald cypress.
All about the woods were warning signs: *Fakahatchee panther*—
          glistening bodies   hidden in the rich
                    thick glade.

I've entered the urban island: angled forest red-
                    shouldered with dust.
               Cabs squeal their native cry—
          Love and *soul* as flinty and loud
                              as a car horn to me now.

Light rain smacks
a black plastic bag flat on the macadam:
               blank face, full of water . . .   like me, like me.

               Barred owl, I'm ready.

Convince me of eternity.

Notes

"Caliban's Ambien Ad" is a found poem. All phrases are taken from either Caliban's speeches in *The Tempest* or the Ambien website.

"Sheep's Lament" was written as a response poem to Sylvia Plath's "Sheep in Fog."

About the Author

Lexa Hillyer received her BA in English from Vassar College and her MFA in Poetry from Stonecoast at the University of Southern Maine. She was the recipient of the Inaugural Poetry Prize from *Tusculum Review* and the First Prize in Poetry from *Brick & Mortar Review*, and was named one of the "Best New Poets of 2012" by Matthew Dickman. Hillyer worked as an editor at both Harper Collins and Penguin, and is co-founder of boutique literary incubator Paper Lantern Lit. She lives in Brooklyn with her husband and a very skinny orange tree.

About Bona Fide Books

The Melissa Lanitis Gregory Poetry Prize was created in memory of Lake Tahoe artist Melissa Gregory, the inspiration for Bona Fide Books. The prize is awarded annually for an unpublished collection of poetry. The winner receives a cash prize, publication, and a reading at Lake Tahoe.

Bona Fide Books is a small press on a mountaintop connecting writers with their readers.

www.bonafidebooks.com

This book is set in Perpetua and Trajan Pro.

Thomson-Shore, our printer, is a member of the Green Press Initiative (GPI) dedicated to environmentally sound publishing. This book is printed on 30% post-consumer recycled paper, processed chlorine free.